Whose Addiction Is It Anyway?

A Mother's Journey of Taking Control and Letting Go

CATHY ALESSANDRA

Copyright 2017 Cathy Alessandra
All rights reserved. No part of this publication may be reproduced, distributed, or transmitted in any form or by any means, including photocopying, recording, or other electronic or mechanical methods, or by any information storage and retrieval system, without prior written permission of the author, except in the case of a brief quotation embodied in reviews and certain other noncommercial uses permitted by copyright law.
ISBN-13: 9781536917956
ISBN-10: 1536917958

Cathy Alessandra
Alessandra Group LLC
46-E Peninsula Center, #403
Rolling Hills Estates, CA 90274
Cover photo courtesy of Cynthia Olkie, Fleur De Lis Photography

Dedicated to the millions of people around the world who are touched by addiction. Whether you're an active addict, a recovering addict, the child of an addict, or a family member or friend of an addict, this story is a reminder that you are not alone.

TABLE OF CONTENTS

Preface		vii
1	Once Upon a Time … It's No Fairy Tale	1
2	The Five Stages: A Roller Coaster Ride to Hell and Back	9
3	Taking Control and Letting Go	17
4	Now What? Tools for You	27
5	A Dad's Perspective, by Dave Cooke	39
6	Tough Love: My Most Excruciating Night as a Parent, by Michelle Rose Gilman	53
7	Where Is God?	59
8	The Counselor's Couch: A Professional Perspective	73
9	Living Sober: A Prescription for Life	81
Final Thoughts and Moving Forward		89
Appendix: Resources		95
Connect with Cathy		97

PREFACE

A Message from Cathy

I started this book in November 2015. I thought, "I got this, I understand it, I've overcome it, and I have to share it." After I completed the first draft, it sat. It was saved, and I had big plans to publish it—but something held me back from finishing. Little did I know at that time it was because I needed to get back in the trenches, sit in the crap, and experience addiction and codependency again to really see it, feel it, and understand it and myself better.

I spent the first half of 2016 in the chaos of codependency. Now keep in mind, addiction isn't just alcohol and chemical dependency. It's dependency on love, food, gambling, sex, shopping, video games and social media…and yes, alcohol and drugs. Only in succumbing to the chaos of trying to "fix it" again did I realize that I had yet again entered into a codependent relationship.

I spent the remainder of 2016 in self-reflection and recovery. Digging into my past, I was able to understand my cycle of "fixing it". It had happened numerous times, going all the way back to childhood. Becoming aware of that in my personality, I am better able to cope and manage my part in various relationships.

While I already had my life-coaching certification, I began pursuing a career in the field of addiction. I became a Certified Professional Recovery Coach and am studying to become a

Certified Alcohol & Drug Counselor (CADC) in the State of California.

Addiction is a disease of the brain. It is not bad people doing bad things. It's a disease that affects people from all walks of life, all ages, all races, all genders, all religions, all parts of the world, and all socioeconomic areas. It is not something that impacts only the very wealthy or the homeless. It touches everyone in between too. Addiction does not discriminate.

If you are reading this, you are no doubt touched by one of the three million addicts in the United States or possibly one of the millions more around the world. This book tells the story of my journey and the stories of a few others as well. It also includes some ideas and concepts on addiction. And lastly, it offers tools and resources I myself have used. Most importantly, it is meant to help you understand that you are not alone. Many of us face this challenge in our lives.

I am grateful that my journey took me to those dark places and brought me back out into the light. I am grateful that I discovered what I truly believe is my purpose and mission—to work to remove the stigma and shame of addiction, *any* addiction. You may wonder about the following phrase in this book's subtitle: *Taking Control and Letting Go*. The fact is, I needed to take control of my own life—my actions, reactions, and recovery—and that meant letting go of trying to control others and their circumstances.

This book is finished from a very different headspace than where it began. It is written with a very humble heart full of grace and gratitude.

1

ONCE UPON A TIME ... IT'S NO FAIRY TALE

There I was—standing in my front yard, watching my son being driven away. It was February 1, 2015. Super Bowl Sunday, in fact. I remember because my husband insisted on taking me out to get something to eat after my son left, and the game was playing in the background of the restaurant. I couldn't eat, though. I was numb. I was in shock. I didn't know what to say or do. I wanted to scream and throw things. I wanted to cry and curl up in the fetal position. It felt like my heart had been ripped out. My son had just left for sober living, a request he had made earlier that day. It was the best day and the worst nightmare.

But I'm getting ahead of myself. Let me back up a bit...

I have three fabulous children. Two girls and my boy. I was married at the young age of twenty-two to my high school sweetheart. We had traveled, moved multiple times, and experienced life before our first child was born in 1992. Shortly after my second daughter was born in 1994, we moved back to our childhood community. And in 1996, I was blessed with my third child, my son.

We became immersed in the community. My children attended the Catholic school, and I became a full-time mom. I was room mom, dance mom, drama mom, and football mom. I loved doing things with and for my kids. It was a whirlwind of chaos at times but craziness I thrived on.

High school moved quickly. My oldest child was involved in the dance team and my middle in the theater department. By fall of 2012, our oldest was off to college, my middle daughter was in her senior year of high school, and my son was a sophomore. He was on the football team and seemed to have a nice group of friends. Everything seemed great—until that fateful day in January 2013.

I was presenting a workshop for women entrepreneurs. The night before the retreat began, I opened my "new" laptop, a hand-me-down that had been my son's. He had a new computer, and for my traveling purposes, his laptop had been handed down to me. When I started up the laptop, I found myself in the inbox of one of his social media accounts. And there, staring me in the face, were e-mails between him and friends about getting high with weed. As I scrolled through the multiple messages, I realized his drug usage had been going on for almost six months. I was in shock, to say the least.

I now had two days of leading, teaching, and training a group of entrepreneur women while this discovery would weigh heavily on my mind and before I could deal with it at home. If I'd known then that our family had just gotten on the roller coaster to a crazy, uncomfortable, hideous ride, I may never have come home.

By the time I returned home from the retreat, my husband had already started the conversation with my son, and it had not gone well. My son had compiled folders full of "facts" and presented to us the "benefits" of using weed, how it wasn't bad for you, and how it was actually better than smoking cigarettes. I can't even remember all the reasons. They seemed so absurd. Who had taken my son and replaced him with this boy? Where had I gone wrong? What had I done wrong? Where had I failed?

Then it became clear that others knew. I tried to hide his habit, covering for him. But in reality, he was out there using weed, and other parents clearly already knew. The embarrassment, the shame, the judgment—I felt it all. "Not my child," was all I heard from other parents, making me and my husband feel that we had allowed this to happen in our home. But no, we had not! We were not the home allowing the parties. We were not the parents providing the alcohol. We were active, involved, and supportive.

My son basically started failing school—cutting classes, arriving tardy most days, and expressing no interest in schoolwork. I began worrying about his friends, grades, and whereabouts. We did the typical parent punishments—taking away his phone, cutting his curfew, not allowing him the car. But here's what that did: I couldn't reach him since he had no phone, and I couldn't track him either. Curfew? Some nights he would get so angry at us that he'd just walk out the door and down the street to a friend's waiting car. And his car? We went so far as to put a lock on the steering wheel after he had taken it one night. We had two years of what I would call nothing short of hell.

He was not a bad kid. He was a kid who, like thousands in America, was escaping life by using weed. And while his folder of "facts" told me it didn't affect him, it clearly did. He became a different kid with a personality I didn't recognize or like. He became a kid who had a lazy side beyond words and anger that spilled into every conversation. He became a kid whose life was turned upside down because of his need to smoke weed and eventually experiment with other drugs.

The roller coaster to hell had started the day I came home from that retreat in January 2013. I am a type A personality, and I was going to fix it and fix him. I yelled, I screamed, I begged, I pleaded, I bribed, I threatened, and I came unglued. I went down the dark hole with him, losing myself in the darkness.

Friends didn't understand. They would say, "I'm sure it's just a phase." And they would continue on about how their children would never use drugs. My husband understood me, of course. He was experiencing the same situations as I was with our son. But truthfully, I don't think dads process the situation the same as moms do. I may be wrong, and it may just have been me, but I think moms take it very personally. To us, it's about our babies who came from our wombs. We love and nurture and give our lives to our children. And we start to think, how could we have let this happen? How did we not see it? What does it mean about the kind of mothers we are?

Never mind the fact I had two daughters who were thriving with straight As in AP courses, gaining multiple college acceptances, making lots of friends, and more. The day he left for sober living was one of the most painful days of my life. Why, you ask, when he asked to go? Because it meant, to me in that moment, that I had failed my son. I had failed in the most important job I would ever have—being his mother. And that left me numb. I spent two days in misery. I found myself on his bed crying. I didn't take phone calls, I texted only a couple of my closest friends, I spoke to a counselor, and I had my husband. As I moved through it, I came to realize the gift God had given us in my son making the decision to *ask* for help rather than us having to do an intervention.

And that is where this book really begins. That is where the title came from as well. Whose addiction is it anyway? It became my addiction to save my son. It became my addiction to find his stash, to troll his social media, to track him at every moment, to fix him. It became my addiction to save my son from his choices. And until I came to grips with my addiction to save him—my codependence and enabling behaviors—and *chose* to get off the roller coaster, I would continue on his downward spiral. I had to save myself so I could support him in the way he needed.

In the following chapters, I'll share how I had to take control and ultimately let go. My survival became my priority. I had to literally "let go and let God." Just as using drugs is the user's or abuser's choice, entering a mother's recovery was my choice.

I share this backstory with you to give you context for the next chapters. Without the story you may wonder, who is she to tell me that? What does she know about how I feel?

She is the one who experienced it deep in the trenches. She is the one who had to sit in the muck and dig out of it. She is the one who had to dive deep, become totally vulnerable, and release the guilt, shame, and fear to be able to reclaim her life and, ultimately, become a better mother.

That's who I am. My hope is that this book will help you connect with other parents either through *Mothers with Hope* (www.motherswithhope.org), a local Alcoholics Anonymous (Al-Anon) meeting, or one of the other resources out there for you. There are thousands of parents in these same circumstances. As I speak more publicly about my story, I am continually connected to others suffering in silence.

Here is the most important takeaway from the whole book; if you learn nothing else, hear this:

You are not alone. We are in this together.

2

THE FIVE STAGES: A ROLLER COASTER RIDE TO HELL AND BACK

As a mother who went through this roller coaster ride, I can only liken it to the five stages of grief. I experienced every stage—some stages lasted longer than others, some were more painful than the previous, but all of them were what I had to experience to get through to the other side of taking control and letting go.

Grief is an uncomfortable thing and it shows up in many places. It doesn't take death to experience it either. A loss is a loss, but to work through anything painful, it does take moving through the stages. Everyone will move at his or her own pace—you can't force it, you can't speed it along. It's a process that will take however much time is needed. You may even go through stages one, two, and three and think you are moving through, only to find yourself back at stage one. By processing through each stage at your own pace, time, and space, you will get to the other side and find peace.

Stage 1: Denial

If I had a penny for every time I've heard "not my child," I'd be a very rich woman! I'm sure there had been signs and symptoms I'd missed. I'm sure I was one of those "not my child" moms at some point. Denial is easy, cheap, and quick, but denial serves no one. Denial is the shock absorber for the soul, protecting us until we become equipped to cope with reality.

Denial is the first stage and what every parent experiences. My family and I lived in a community where it seemed everyone was in denial. Everyone acted as if his or her child was the only one not participating in these experiences in high school—not drinking, not using drugs—and he or she would be forcefully adamant. I'm sure I was too—in the beginning.

While I always hoped my children were not involved, I'm sure I played the denial game well, like the rest of the moms. I cherished the very open relationship I had with my daughters. While I'm sure they didn't tell me everything, they certainly told me a lot. I did a lot of listening and tried to contain my utter surprise as things were shared. You know, holding that poker face as you are dying inside.

When things started to get out of control with my son, it was clear that many had known what was going on, yet no one had said a thing. After finding those messages on his social media account, I was no longer in denial. I had to face the facts and figure out what was next.

Denial is the first phase—it's also one of the most difficult phases. To admit there is a problem is to admit there is a breakdown somewhere. Denial is a coping mechanism to buffer what we don't want to see but is usually there in plain sight. However, when something happens that no longer allows denial, like the messages I read, or a DUI, or something worse, denial moves quickly into the next phase—anger.

Stage 2: Anger

Anger is ugly and can be destructive, but it's also a necessary step through healing. And let me tell you, I was angry! How could my son do this to me? How could God let this happen? How could my friends abandon me?

I had a temper—I admit it. And the anger bubbling inside of me after the denial was, at times, rage. I had been the mother I was "supposed" to be. I'd been to his cub scout meetings and soccer games, I'd attended every football game and cheered him on, I'd supported his love of dirt bikes and riding, I'd chaperoned field trips, I had birthday parties in every theme he loved, and I'd loved him through a particularly difficult time in middle school. And now he was doing this to me?

I was angry, humiliated, embarrassed, and guilty, and I was also asking, "Why me?" What had I done wrong? I had two older daughters who had thrived through school. Where had I gone wrong with my son?

That was my first problem. I was trying to figure out through my anger how this was my fault. I'd made it about me. But the fact was it had nothing, or very little, to actually do with me. My come-to-Jesus moment was on a Saturday afternoon when my son and I got into a verbal fight—a common occurrence in those days. He had something of mine I wanted—and he was not about to give it up. I went to grab it, and the next thing I knew, I was on the floor with him screaming in my face like I had never heard. I said nothing. I didn't react or scream back. It was probably the most sobering moment of my life, understanding the incredible pain he was in and not being able to fix it, change it or make it go away.

Anger is a stage we must go through to journey toward the light. We get angry at the user/addict, we get angry at our spouse or significant other, and we get angry at teachers, friends, family, and God. Anger can take many forms. I took my anger out on others, and I took it out on myself. But being in the place of anger and sitting through the pain, I discovered more about myself and my son.

Note: I recently had a conversation with my son about that Saturday afternoon fight. When I inquired, he didn't remember it. Any of it. I know he never would have physically hurt me. That moment was him hurting and raging within himself, and I happened to put myself in the way.

Stage 3: Bargaining

After that Saturday afternoon, my anger had subsided. I understood my son's extreme anger and pain, and I wanted to help fix it or save him. That is when the bargaining began.

If I could save him, there was hope. I backed off on the requirement of total sobriety. Instead of anger and disdain, I showed love and empathy. However, I let the boundaries slip. If he smoked only once in a week, he could drive the car to school. If he went to school, I wouldn't check on his grades. If he checked in with me while he was out, he could have his phone. However, it never worked.

My expectations in bargaining were never met. I was willing to self-sacrifice to bargain with the devil. During my bargaining phase, my son had the upper hand, even though I thought I did. The fact was, since I wanted to fix him, I didn't fully see, or want to see, all that was continuing to go on.

Stage 4: Depression

I don't think I fully went into depression until my son moved into sober living and treatment. You may ask, "Why *then*?" He'd asked for help, he himself had called his counselor and asked to go immediately, but I felt I had failed. I had not been able to save him. I had not been able to make a difference. As his mother, the one who had given him life, who had loved him so deeply, I was not able to make it all better.

I spent the first three days of his sober living nestled in my bed, on his bed, and on the couch. I couldn't think, eat, pray, or talk. I cried. I was numb. I had never experienced anything like that before, and I hope to never experience anything like it again. In looking back, I'm grateful to my husband for his patience and understanding. I'm grateful to my friends for understanding that I couldn't even talk on the phone and that communicating via text message was about all I could handle. I am most grateful for the two women who showed up on my doorstep on day three and quite literally picked me up. They showed up and worked remotely from my house—so that I wasn't alone.

My depression lasted a few more weeks, though not at the deep dark place it had started. I began to understand that what I had prayed for all along had happened. In reality, the day my son had asked to go to sober living was the same day my husband and I had coordinated with the counselor to hold an intervention the following weekend.

I'd been on my way to a hair appointment (yes, the gray was showing with all the stress). We'd had a conference call with my son's counselor and agreed that the following Saturday we'd hold an intervention. During the rest of my drive, about an hour, I thought about how I'd make some of his favorite meals and would do a couple of extra things for him during the week. I was preparing for his departure, but that all ended abruptly when *he* made the decision. He'd yet again changed plans without warning, but in reflecting on the turn of events,

I realize it was God's way of releasing me. We had made the decision, and in my heart, I believe God said, "No worries, Cathy. You have released him. You have let go. Now let Me ease your pain." Yes, my Higher Power is God—and my faith is strong. So I now believe in my heart that's how it happened.

Depression is something we must work through. It is just another step in the journey of recovery. For me, depression meant total hopelessness. It was giving up. Unfortunately, it's a required part of the process. There isn't a way to avoid it, but there are tools to help you move through it more easily. I attended support groups, reached out to friends, prayed, and kept moving forward—if even just a baby step every single day.

Stage 5: Acceptance—let go and let God

Acceptance takes time. I had been working through my stages of grief for a couple of years. It came in stages as he moved through his stages of use, abuse, and recovery. As I began to accept the path, I began to understand this wasn't my journey and it was time to focus on my recovery.

I had spent much of my time trying to save him. I had spent a lot of time on trying to fix the problem. I had become codependent—trying to not enable him but, in reality, becoming a big enabler. This is where things dramatically changed in my life. By accepting his path, accepting him, and loving him unconditionally with no expectations, then—and only then—could I begin healing me.

I remind myself every day that I must let go and let God. This is my son's journey with consequences he must face. I am here to love him unconditionally, but unconditionally doesn't mean without boundaries.

These five stages will take time. They aren't something you can rush and, in fact, you may even move back and forth between them. But it's very clear that until you really process the stages, work through them, not rush through them, you can't get to the acceptance phase. I have a mantra I use a lot, and it's even on a sticky note on my computer screen. It saves me when I begin to go into that dark hole, and it is a constant reminder of who really is in charge…

Surrender, accept, and pray.

3

TAKING CONTROL AND LETTING GO

We had counselors for my son during this period of time—multiple counselors. In June 2013, we finally found one who connected with him. This counselor was different in his approach. There was no sitting on a couch for an hour in an office once a week. He preferred on-the-go sessions, meeting my son outdoors or for a meal. It was one-to-two hours each week, plus group sessions. In November 2013, the counselor posed a question to me that started my journey into recovery. It was a question that opened my mind and heart to realizing I needed to take care of me before I could become the parent my son needed.

Shortly after that conversation, I found myself in Santa Barbara for a business retreat. During that retreat, I decided to stay for an additional twenty-four hours by myself. No phone. No TV. No computer or e-mail. That was not an easy task for me! Instead, I picked up a book: *The Four Agreements,* by don Miguel Ruiz. If you haven't read it, now is the time to do so! It's an amazing book. A life-changing book for me. Actually, a life-saving book.

The Four Agreements and their definitions, as written by don Miguel Ruiz, are as follows:

1. Be impeccable with your word: Speak with integrity. Say only what you mean. Avoid using the Word to speak against yourself or to gossip about others. Use the power of your Word in the direction of truth and love.
2. Do not take things personally: Nothing others do is because of you. What others say and do is a projection

of their own reality, their own dream. When you are immune to the opinions and actions of others, you won't be the victim of needless suffering.
3. Never make assumptions: Find the courage to ask questions and to express what you really want. Communicate with others as clearly as you can to avoid misunderstandings, sadness and drama. With just this one agreement, you can completely transform your life.
4. Always do your best: Your best is going to change from moment to moment; it will be different when you are healthy as opposed to sick. Under any circumstance, simply do your best, and you will avoid self-judgment, self-abuse, and regret.

It was a powerful book, with ideas and concepts I related to and knew would shift my life. When I started relating those four agreements to the things that were going on in my life, I realized that I was not living by those agreements whatsoever.

Be impeccable with your word; I interpreted that to mean not only the gossip and talking about others, but also that little voice inside my head that would constantly say to me, "Who do you think you are? You can't do that. You're not good enough. You're not smart enough. You have failed as a parent." It also meant thinking before I spoke and responding, not reacting.

Do not take things personally; I was taking a lot of things personally. I think as women we do, right? We're defined by our children and their actions—at least I was. My son wasn't doing this to hurt me personally. It was his battle. I had made it all about me and, in reality, it had very little to do with me at all! There are a lot of things we take personally, or at least that I was taking personally, and that agreement alone would make a tremendous difference in my life.

Never make assumptions; it was time for me to ask the tough questions and clearly express my feelings. I was making a lot of assumptions in various areas of my life. I needed to ask questions and not assume anything anymore.

And the final agreement, *always do your best.* My interpretation of this agreement was that those first three agreements were hard to live by. They were big, tall orders to live life 24/7, but if I could do my best to live within those four agreements every day then maybe it would help me to change some of the circumstances I was experiencing.

I knew it was time for a change. In understanding these four agreements, I realized that if I made some changes and shifted my life to follow the four agreements, I could potentially change my circumstances and, at least, change my own life. I couldn't control anybody else's life, but I could control mine. I had to save myself, I had to take care of me, and I had to put myself through recovery—whole-life recovery: mind, body, and spirit. I came back that November morning from Santa Barbara a different person.

I was now committed to making some changes, from my health to my business, from my marriage to my son. He needed to make his own choices, and he was going to have his own consequences for those choices, which he did. There was nothing I could do, and it wasn't my fault. All the taking it personally, which is exactly what I was doing, was literally killing me. I had to exit the roller coaster, and let him ride it alone—not an easy choice for a mother who wants to protect her family at all costs.

I had been fully attached—to my son, to the expectations of others, and to the outcome. I was swirling in my own head and totally out of control. I had to regain control *of my life*, no one else's. I did this by finding my mantra—*yes I can*—and using it all the time. Yes I Can is a whole movement of transformation—and a different book I wrote (www.TheYesICanBook.com). My time of silence and solitude in Santa Barbara along with committing to living by the four agreements was the turning point of my life in many ways. Finding my mantra was truly a divine intervention.

In reflecting how I was able to take control of my own life, I discovered three pillars. These pillars were critical to my whole life recovery. They are self-care, sacred space, and support.

Let me elaborate on each.

Pillar #1: Self-care

This is where the instructions about first putting on your oxygen mask before putting on your child's rings true! If you are not healthy in mind, body, and spirit, facing the challenges of addiction will become even more overwhelming. Self-care begins with self-love and self-worth. We cannot love anyone else until we truly love ourselves, unconditionally. And we have a hard time loving ourselves if we don't have self-worth or self-value.

How do we experience self-care? First, we have to stop taking care of everyone else, and take care of ourselves. It's about making you the number-one priority. It's about doing whatever it takes and making sure you schedule it into your day, week, month, year, and life.

Self-care includes mental, physical, and spiritual health. My mental health is nurtured with self-discovery and reflection. My physical health is nurtured by healthy foods and exercise. My spiritual health is fed by prayer and meditation. Let's take a look at a couple of core areas and how you can make them work for you.

- *Health.* What are you willing to commit to for self-care? Going to the gym? Taking a walk…daily? Eating healthy foods? Reading, meditating, or journaling?
- *Relationships.* Relationships require self-care. In yearning for deeper connections, I attended workshops and read books on my own. I worked on things from my side. I couldn't change others, but I could change the way I saw the circumstances and how I responded. I made time and became fully present.
- *Spirituality.* My relationship with God has never been stronger. I had grown up in a home where God was important, but until I began down this path of self-destruction, I had not fully connected with my faith. Yes, I went to church—but goes much deeper then attending a service each week. God is with me, and He is for me. I truly believe my journey is guided by Him—including the dark, ugly moments. While I want to run and hide from the difficulties of life, and I admit I still do, I also know that these are the times of greatest growth, and

> I am trusting God for the lesson. My self-care includes nurturing my relationship with God, daily, by praying, reading, listening, journaling, and serving.

Self-care takes massive doses of love, courage, forgiveness, and empathy. There is nothing selfish about self-care. We cannot be the best person we are meant to be if we don't do the "work" on ourselves. This can mean peeling back layers of old stories from our past, digging into why we are holding on to them, and then doing the work to move through them to create new and healthy experiences.

For me, this meant starting with my health and becoming aware of my mindless numbing tactics, which included stuffing my feelings in the form of food. It meant creating a ritual for time with God every morning, no matter what. It meant loving myself, forgiving myself, and understanding I am not perfect and that is ok, as long as I am doing my best.

Pillar #2: Sacred Space

Sacred space is about physical, emotional, relational, and virtual space. It's about boundaries. It's about finding yourself in and surrounding yourself by a space that fills your soul.

- *Physical space.* What do you have in your physical sacred space – your bedroom, office, or car? Do you have a place in your garden where you can get away and escape? Sometimes we need to get out of our immediate physical space and move to the greater expanse by getting in nature.

In my home, I have inspirational paintings, my vision board, and pictures of my family. On my back patio, I've created a sacred space with a fountain and flowers where I can escape to write, meditate or pray. I created a space to feel safe and nurtured. How can you create a physical space that will fill your soul?

- *Emotional space.* When we are in the depths of despair, many of us isolate ourselves or disappear. We don't take calls, don't go out, and don't leave our rooms or homes. Emotional space is important to honor as we work through life's difficulties. With that said, it's important to put emotional boundaries in place, but it's also important to not push everything and everyone out of the emotional space. Going through life's difficulties is not meant to be done all alone with no support. (More on that in Pillar #3.)
- *Relational space.* Facing any crisis puts a large strain on any relationship. Whether you are married, divorced, or a single parent, each of us will react differently. It's important to understand what space you need, what space your significant other needs, and how you both can get your needs met. Like me, some people need more connection. Others need more distance. Both are ok if we have learned self-care and have the tools to find the space and support we need to face the crisis.
- *Virtual space.* In this world of virtual everything, it's important to remember to create virtual space as well. E-mail, social media, text messages, and more, can be

difficult to face as you are facing this crisis in your family. Put boundaries in place.

Pillar #3: Support

Support is the glue that holds it all together. We cannot do it alone, period! While we need to experience and process some of this alone, we cannot *do* it alone. We need the support of our family, friends, counselors, coaches, therapists, and more. I had support in every area of my life.

I had girlfriends, guy friends, a significant other, counselors, coaches, therapists, and mentors, and the list goes on. While I had the dark days of isolation, I also had those whom I could reach out to and lean on or those who would check on me.

It's important to look for support in the right places. Not everyone has earned the right to be in your inner circle while you're in a crisis. I experienced great shame while processing all of this. I needed to lean on and rely on those who would not judge me, who would just listen and not try to fix it, and who would just be with me.

Letting Go

Letting go. I can only imagine what is going through your mind. "Let go? Are you kidding me?" But here is the truth for me: Only by letting go—of my son, my expectations, my shame, and the judgment—only by letting go was I truly able to save myself and reach him.

I tried everything I could to fix the situation. I tried everything I could to fix him and to fix me. I tried to fix my marriage, my friendships, my business, and my life. And I couldn't fix a single one of those. I could only help myself be the best that I could be by letting go of guilt, shame, expectations, judgment, and more. I surrendered. I accepted. I let go and let God. And only in doing that was I able to begin the healing process.

Do I continue to struggle with surrender? Of course, I'm human. But I'm aware of it and practice these things daily, sometimes moment-by-moment as the dark clouds appear. Letting go was the hardest thing I have ever done, but it has changed my life in a multitude of ways.

Whole-Life Recovery
What is Whole Life Recovery? A process that heals the mind, body, and spirit. It's peeling back the layers of your mind and understanding what drives you, what motivates you, why you see the world the way you do, and how you can make the necessary shifts for a positive, fulfilling, joy-filled life that allows for unconditional self-love and love of others. It's taking care of your body—a vessel not to be abused but to be nurtured with food, movement, sleep, and more. It's feeding your spirit and finding a deeper connection and relationship with your Higher Power through meditation, prayer, silence, and solitude.

By taking the time to work through your own whole life recovery, you will be better able to be present in all areas of your life.

4

NOW WHAT? TOOLS FOR YOU

Addiction is a family affair. Everyone is involved, even if only one person is addicted. A parent might wonder what he or she can do to fix it. A sibling might be pressured to cover for his or her brother or sister. When I began to live by *The Four Agreements* and practice self-love, I shifted my life. My attitude changed. I wasn't as easily triggered, I began to understand I wasn't in control, and I focused on myself and how I was managing my expectations and expressions. I was also able to provide support, love, and empathy for the other family members involved.

So, what can you do?

Get the facts
To deal with any problem effectively in life, we must first try to understand it as best we can. The answer to "What should I do?" depends on many factors, including family dynamics, age, substance, and more. Statistics show that over 75 percent of American children under age eighteen have used alcohol, smoked marijuana, or tried other drugs. Drugs do not discriminate based on age, location, gender, or financial status. Teens use drugs and alcohol for a variety of reasons: to escape, to numb, to fit in with peers, and more. Drugs are used to enhance pleasure or escape reality.

Although there are many reasons an adolescent begins using drugs or alcohol, including medical and genetic predispositions, the use of these substances carry known consequences. Using drugs or alcohol can halt emotional development and severely harm physical, social, and mental development.

I give a presentation to parents, called "Not My Child: The Sobering Facts of Use, Abuse, and Addiction." Not every child who uses drugs or alcohol will become an abuser or addict. What makes one child respond to drugs in an abusive way while another child is able to use them occasionally and remain nonabusive? The scientific answer is for psychologists, psychiatrists, and the professionals to provide. But as a mom, here are my opinions of the various levels of use and what they may look like:

Use: experiential/experimental/social
Use is experiential, experimental and driven by social influences. This is where peer pressure comes in. "Everyone is doing it." I've heard that hundreds of times. The child wants to experiment and experience it—what does it do, how does it make me feel, who can I impress? They may try drinking or doing drugs. They may experiment with weed or hard-core drugs. They may attend a pill or "skittles party," where everyone drops his or her parents' prescription drugs into a large bowl and then picks out random ones and takes them.

They are invincible. They don't believe they can be hurt or injured or that they can become addicted. They don't look at the bigger consequences. They just want to give it a try like all their friends. The motto is this: be accepted and be cool.

Abuse: dependency or the need of it to feel better

When does it become abuse? In my opinion, the minute the user needs the substance to feel better. Research findings I have read talk again and again about lack of confidence and self-esteem as being the catalyst for continued use and abuse. Abusers begin using on a regular basis—sometimes daily, sometimes multiple times a day. It's no longer the occasional Friday night with friends—it's even when they are alone.

Addiction: can't live without it

When does it cross from abuse to dependency or addiction? When the addict can't live or cope without it. It becomes his or her waking thought—how will they get it, when can they get it, and who can they get it from? Getting the next fix becomes an obsession.

When considering treatment or support for your family, the answer to "What should I do?" may vary. You may reach out to friends or other family members for advice, but even then, differing opinions may send you into deeper confusion.

I encourage parents to do their "research." This may mean reading books, consulting with professionals, asking trusted friends for referrals and resources, and following your gut. When my child was in the thick of it, we were bombarded with various options, with many people suggesting we send him to a "wilderness" program. However, my husband and I just didn't feel that it was the best option for our child. It is successful for many other families, but for our son, it was not the best option.

Reach out to the many resources in your community and get informed about the options. Step out of your child's chaos; understand he/she is not doing this *to* you; understand how deep into use, abuse, or addiction your child has fallen; and decide what is best for your family from a place of knowledge and love, not fear and panic.

Are you enabling?
"Enabling" is when a family member or other person close to the addict facilitates, and therefore encourages/supports his or her continued behaviors by not holding the addict accountable for his or her actions. This includes covering up or making excuses for them and not setting appropriate boundaries. Family members may begin to take sides rather than coming together as a united front.

Enabling your child only prolongs the addiction. The longer it takes for parents to make the choice to stop "fixing" or rescuing the child, the harder the battle may become.

Here are a few questions to consider:

> Do you loan money to your child but never ask to be paid back?
> Do you repress your anger just to maintain the peace in the family?
> Do you blame yourself for the negative actions of your loved one?

> Do you set boundaries only to let them slide and not enforce them?
> Have you lied to the attendance office at school?

The follow-up question to any of the questions you answered yes to is "Why?" I have done it. I answered yes to all those questions. As an enabler, my purpose was to protect my son and family from the consequences. I thought I was holding things together by walking on eggshells, so as not to cause more discord. But in the meantime, I was losing my mind in anger, frustration, and disappointment.

What about codependency?

The definition of "codependency," per *Wikipedia*, is as follows:

> Codependency is a type of dysfunctional helping relationship where one person supports or enables another person's drug addiction, alcoholism, gambling addiction, poor mental health, immaturity, irresponsibility, or underachievement. Among the core characteristics of codependency, the most common theme is an excessive reliance on other people for approval and a sense of identity. In its broadest definition, a codependent is someone who cannot function from their innate self and whose thinking and behavior is instead organized around another person, or even a process, or substance.

Codependency is a tendency to behave in an overly passive or excessively caretaking way that negatively impacts a person's relationships and quality of life. It usually involves putting one's personal needs at a lower priority than others' on a continuous basis, while being excessively preoccupied with helping others and meeting their needs. It can occur in families, friendships, work, romance, and more. As you can see from the description from Wikipedia, it's not *just* about addiction. This type of behavior can show up in many situations.

There are many resources for codependents, including Codependents Anonymous. I have read and continue to use Melody Beattie's book *The Language of Letting Go*, as a daily reminder. Behaviors of codependency are like an addiction. Becoming aware of and shifting the behavior is critical to everyone involved.

Expectations and setting boundaries

Managing expectations of yourself and others is critical. Being clear with your boundaries is the starting place. Setting boundaries allows for a clear understanding of what is acceptable—and what is not.

Boundaries are physical and relational. They need to be put into place and followed. When considering boundaries, it's important to be clear about expectations and consequences. It's important to communicate the boundary in a calm, rational manner—not in the heat of an argument or crisis. First, when communicating the boundary, you explain what will no longer be tolerated. Next, communicate the consequence of the boundary being crossed. Lastly, describe what you will do to protect and enforce that boundary.

As parents, we are stopped many times from setting and following through with boundaries and consequences because of fear. We fear he or she may walk out, disappear, end up in jail, have no friends, dive deeper into drug use, or even choose to end his or her life. Keep in mind, however, that anyone who is dependent on drugs or alcohol will do or say anything to maintain a cover-up and continue his or her addiction.

The purpose of boundaries is also to take care of you and the rest of the family. No one deserves to be treated poorly. No one deserves to be a victim of an addict. Setting boundaries, communicating expectations, holding firmly, and following through with consequences are the first steps to owning your strength as the parent.

Managing your emotions

This is a highly emotionally charged situation for all. As a mother, I felt shame, guilt, judgment, fear, and stress. Remember, however, it's not them doing it to you.

Acknowledging your feelings and finding an outlet is important. Awareness is critical and gives you the opportunity to respond, not react. I can't begin to share how in my fits of rage I would certainly react in a way that was truly hurtful in the long run for my son. I have no doubt that my negative feelings and reactions toward him would bring on more feelings of anger and guilt for him—potentially driving him to find more escape in the drug.

It takes courage to take a step back in the heat of the moment, a self-imposed time-out, if you will. Take a breath, even walk away, until cooler heads can prevail. Some suggestions for managing emotions include the following:

- *Awareness of negative emotions.* How does your child push your buttons? What are your triggers? How do you usually respond, and what can you do to respond more constructively?
- *Self-imposed time-out.* When constructive conversation is giving way to a fight, give yourself permission for a time-out. Our counselor suggested this for all of us, even my son. When the heat begins to rise and it seems that the conversation is headed in a destructive direction, any one of us could call a time-out and walk away. It is not easy, but it can help to diffuse the situation.
- *Find outlets to release your feelings.* I got to the point where I would literally get up and walk out the door. I needed fresh air, a walk, the gym, or a phone call to a friend. One day I will never forget is the day I received a phone call that delivered bad news, again. I thought I was going to come unglued. I remember giving in to about two minutes of rage before I caught myself in the downward spiral and turned it around by searching for the nearest, soonest Al-Anon meeting. That was a turning point for me—searching for and getting support from those who could understand.
- *Continued self-care.* When we are tired, stressed, and off-balance, our resilience can and will falter. It's important to take time for self-care. It may seem like the

last thing you should do, but only in taking care of yourself can you be the best person or mother. This means getting enough sleep, eating a healthy diet, and exercising daily—even if that means taking a walk just around the block. It also means spending time with those who fill you up: friends, family, and a significant other. Allow others to pour into you—supporting you with hugs, laughs, and a safe space to share.

Support for family members
Addiction involves the whole family. Everyone suffers. If there are siblings, particularly if they are living at home, it's important to tend to their emotional needs. The stress on them to cover for the addict sibling or make excuses for him or her at school can become overwhelming. Providing a safe space for them to share their fears, anxieties, and anger is helpful for them to let go.

Forgiveness
Love yourself unconditionally. As parents, we do the best we can. We blame ourselves and others. But playing the blame game is like drinking the poison. When we blame the friends, the school, the other parent, or worse yet, ourselves, we are holding on to negative emotions rather than moving into acceptance. By holding on to the blame and all the negative emotions that go along with it, we are only hurting ourselves internally. Stress, anger, depression, and the like take a toll on our bodies and health. If you can forgive and understand this isn't anyone's fault, you will be in a place of empowered strength to support your child as needed.

Surrender, accept, and pray

Until you truly understand you can't fix this and it isn't your journey, you will continue in the chaos with the addict. It's important for families to remember that the addict is not doing this to them, that he or she is not bad, and that he or she can regain his or her life.

Get honest about the addiction. Get the facts. Don't blame or try to fix the problem. Get with God or your Higher Power. I was reminded to surrender, accept, and pray. Surrender to my expectations, fears, and concerns. Accept the crisis as it was. And pray for peace, safety, and wholeness. My personal prayer was and is this: God, grant me faith in the darkness, peace in the chaos, hope in the despair, and comfort in knowing I am not alone.

Al-Anon's three Cs helped me understand that I didn't **C**ause it, I can't **C**ontrol it, and I can't **C**ure it. The one thing we can control is how we respond, and not react.

Your daily choice

Whether the addict taking the drug, the family member enabling the act, or the codependent losing himself or herself in excessive caretaking, everyone makes a daily choice. You can live in fear and self-sacrifice, you can live in guilt and shame, you can live allowing the feelings of judgment, depression, and the like to rule your life—or not. The choice is yours.

Just like the user/abuser/addict, *you* have a choice to use the "drug" or stay clean. You have the choice of whether to get entangled and enmeshed with the addict, or not. You have the choice of whether to love with empathy and understanding and set boundaries, or not.

You cannot do this alone
You cannot do this alone. That is the bottom line. No one can go through this alone—not the dependent person or the family. The help of counselors, friends, significant others, therapists, professionals, and support groups are a critical piece to the recovery for all.

5

A DAD'S PERSPECTIVE, BY DAVE COOKE

Note from Cathy: Although I am a mother, I felt it was important to have the perspective of a father. I happened to connect online with Dave Cooke and knew he was just the person.

Dave is the father of a son battling heroin addiction. He has been on this journey since 2009 and is all too familiar with the impact that addiction has on a family. In the early stages of this experience, he was nearly destroyed financially, professionally, and personally. If it weren't for the successful achievement of a cycling challenge he gave himself—one hundred consecutive days of riding, at least one hour a day—who knows where he would have been. Today, he knows his son's story is not his story nor is it his story to tell. Rather, Dave's story is about faith, love, and grace and how God guides him through the most difficult experiences to discover a place of peace, clarity, and purpose. His is a powerful story, and I am grateful he was willing to share…

Q: When and how did you realize your son was using drugs or alcohol?

A: That's an interesting question. As I reflect on my journey, I had three opportunities to come to some understanding that my son was dealing with drugs and alcohol. The first was when he was about fourteen years old. I came home from work early; he was just coming in from the back-deck porch, having smoked a joint. I caught him by surprise—he was a little bit shocked to see me. Being that I was a child of the '70s and a pretty active user, I did not pay a whole lot of attention to the issue. I talked to him a little bit but was rather dismissive of this event as a sign of an issue. I probably spent a little bit less time on it than, in hindsight, I could have.

About four or five years later, my wife informed me that my son was being treated for an OxyContin dependency, and he was getting treatment for this addiction. It didn't really register with me what that meant. Because my wife seemed to have it under control and had it all figured out, I didn't pay a whole lot of attention to it. I just trusted that whatever was going on was being handled.

About a year-and-a-half later, I got a phone call from my son, who at the time was living in San Francisco, telling me that he was going to move back to his hometown of Detroit to enter rehab because he had relapsed and the issue was an addiction to heroin. He was moving back to Detroit because that was where he wanted to get help.

Again, the word "addiction" didn't really register with me then as much as it would today because I did not understand what that word really meant. When I did get that phone call that he was dealing with his addiction, I figured that because he was dealing with it that it wasn't a serious problem. Instead it was something that was actually going to be handled, fixed, and taken care of.

Q: At what point did you realize it had gone from using to abusing? Was there a specific situation?
A: I finally realized the severity of my son's drug abuse and addiction when I got a call from my daughter, who was on vacation visiting friends and family in Detroit. She called to let me know that my son was in jail. As the story unfolded and we tried to better understand why my son was in jail, we found

out that he had been homeless shortly after he moved back to Detroit; and, as a result of a series of addiction-related arrests, he had ditched his court dates and there was an open warrant for his arrest. He was in jail for these offenses, and addiction was running his life.

That was when I finally realized this was a much more serious issue. With this enlightenment, I went into action as a dad to save my kid. That's when I finally realized this addiction thing was serious. This was an issue where his life had been affected, and that's when I understood the difference between using (i.e., just getting high) versus abusing and becoming addicted, where the behaviors were resulting in life-impacting events.

Q: Do you believe your son is an addict whether or not he does?
A: My son would tell you he absolutely, positively has an addiction. He does not shy away from it. He is definitely not in denial of it. Once one recognizes he or she has an addiction, especially an addiction like heroin, the challenge is understanding how much work and effort is involved and how slippery the recovery/relapse slope is. And with every relapse, there is usually a life-changing or life-altering event that precedes or follows it.

Unfortunately, some parents lose their children to a life event that's called "overdose." But with my son's continuous string of arrests, his life event is that he becomes further and further behind the eight ball of the legal system.

Do I think my son is an addict? I don't like to use that word and wouldn't call him one. My son suffers from an addiction. His addiction has taken over his life. And it's taken over his life in the sense that his freedoms have slowly but systematically been taken away from him.

These are freedoms and opportunities to do the things he loves to do. They impact things like his health and his financial situation and other areas of his life. With every relapse, he goes backward and loses his freedom. He is definitely addicted to his drug and it is a serious issue.

Q: How did *you* personally deal with the potential feelings of anger, disappointment, humiliation, guilt, hopelessness—or any other feelings you might have experienced?
I can tell you I have experienced all of those things. I think when my son was in jail is when I first realized how serious his issue was. I was so shocked and saddened to think of my little guy, that bright light of a kid who was so much fun to be around. It was devastating to think he could possibly be in a situation where he was addicted to a drug like heroin and was spending time in jail.

It broke me and made me sad. I immediately went into rescue mode. I was going to save my boy. I was going to get him back to that place where he could start over again.

As far as the word "guilt," yes there is definitely guilt. As I talked about in the first question, I suddenly realized that as a dad I was so focused on things that were important to me, that I had minimized things that could have been warning signs from my son.

I definitely felt guilty and I think that my rescue mission was a by-product of my guilt. I may have missed signals that allowed him to end up on the slippery slope of his addiction; but if it's not too late, I still can save him. I'm sure that my initial responses stemmed from my feelings of guilt.

When it comes to disappointment, more than anything else, it's just the disappointment that my son can't figure it out. It's so disappointing and frustrating to discover that an addiction can be so strong and powerful they can't find or embrace a sustained recovery. It's confounding and confusing.

I gave up alcohol fifteen years ago. I gave up alcohol by making a decision that I wanted my life to be better. I challenged myself at the urging of a psychologist to give up drinking, and I did because I wanted my life to be better. And for me it was just a simple matter of making that decision and sticking to it.

I went through the whole process of being perpetually disappointed that my son couldn't make as simple a decision as I did. It wasn't until I understood how serious his addiction was, or the extent to which the addiction had taken over his life, that I came to realize that sometimes those types of decisions just aren't that simple. It's extremely disappointing to experience every deceitful episode and every relapse; it's also disappointing to think of the times he stole from us or his siblings. Yes, disappointment just reigns supreme.

I am pretty certain I never lost hope, though I was close. What I almost lost was control of my life. I struggled to cope with the chaos in his life. It was to the point where I just didn't think it was possible for me to have peace in my life until my son was better. I became attached to the outcomes of recovery as a measure of success in my life. That is an incredibly powerless place to live.

I guess the bigger question is, "How did you personally deal with this?" There are the things I just dealt with. What his addiction did to me personally was significant. It impacted my business, because all I would do is focus on my son. In my relationships, I simply holed up and hid. I didn't have anything to talk about. There wasn't a whole lot of joy. It didn't do much for me to be distracted by whatever was going on in the family. I was obsessively preoccupied with my son and his behaviors.

It affected my health. I'm a stress eater, and I didn't work out like I could. I gained weight and was physically unhealthy. Plus, I didn't really do a good job of expressing, sharing, or communicating my true emotions with anybody. Instead, I really felt like this was my problem, so I absorbed it internally.

Everything I did was classic crisis mode. I went into crisis mode, holed up, fought the hard battle, and acted as though I had to fight this battle on my own. I didn't even really communicate well with my wife. I just dug in and tried to figure it out. I kept telling myself, "There's got to be a way to save my son. Despite all the stuff he was doing, there's got to be a way to keep getting through this." With every setback and failure, my resolve to stick in a fight intensified. The cost was significant.

Q: At what point, if any, did you realize it was not about you and that you had to let go and let God take over? At that point, what did you do differently?

There was a point where I had that aha moment. It happened in the middle of the night. Whenever my son would disappear or go missing, I would often wake up in the middle of the night and struggle to fall asleep. When that would happen, I would go out on the porch and look up to the sky and just say, "God, wherever my son is just watch over him, and please bring him home safely to me."

And then, I'd pause and look around again and say, "God, please let me find peace in the chaos." Most times, I would go back to bed. But this one night I caught myself saying, "This addiction is destroying me." I realized the extent to which I had become so attached to saving or rescuing my son from an addiction he really wasn't committed to being rescued from. I finally admitted I needed to do something for me before I was lost to his addiction as well.

It was at that point in time that I made a commitment to ride my bike for one hundred days in a row for at least an hour a day. A couple of days later, I started that bike journey. Every day for one hundred days, I rode my bike. Every day I came back from the meditational experiences of the bike ride with clarity about what I knew I needed to do in my life. I knew how I was going to respond to future actions or experiences with an addicted mind.

With every single bike ride and through every single future conflict, I got more clarity, more strength, and more wisdom in dealing with my son's addiction. I got to the point where his addiction stopped taking over my life, and I started getting my life back. That midnight epiphany and the subsequent bike rides were my breakthrough moments.

While I credit my bike rides, I would say for anybody that the breakthrough opportunity comes the moment you realize you have no control over an addiction or the person with the addiction.

Q: What are the top three pieces of advice you would give a parent today, knowing what you know and experiencing it first hand?

The first piece of advice I would offer is to teach your children early to understand, experience, and learn from the consequences of their choices, decisions, and behaviors. Do not protect them from these outcomes.

A parent's responsibility is to nurture, teach, grow, and educate his or her children to the best of his or her ability. Part of the learning experience is to teach your children to understand that for every action, every behavior, and every decision there is an outcome and there is a consequence. Part of the teaching process is to help them at a very, very early age to instill that lesson in them.

As parents, we never want our kids to suffer. We don't want our kids to experience setbacks or failures. We don't want our children to feel disappointment. But every time we do something to soften the blow of the impact of their decisions, we are missing an opportunity to teach them one of life's most important lessons—with every one of our decisions there is going to be an outcome. Things don't always go as we plan or desire. Life isn't always fair. The reality is that stuff happens, and much of the stuff that happens is a result of our decisions. We all need to better understand what those consequences are. We can't learn from them if we don't experience the consequences of our decisions.

The time to instill that lesson is when they're very young, when they are still impressionable. Teaching that lesson later on in life is very difficult. When they are young, they look up to their parents and they listen, watch and observe them. When they're teenagers, they're not listening and learning as much as challenging and testing.

If you have protected or coddled them from the outcomes of their choices or behaviors when they were young, they will not be able to engage in a consequence-based response to addiction-related behaviors. If you have taught them that there's a way out or a way to avoid the consequences, or that there's a rule that should be bent or broken or a punishment that can be interpreted or minimized, you have presented them with a mixed message that will impact them later in life.

When dealing with an addict child, having a rational conversation with an irrational mind is already difficult and challenging. Having that conversation with a mind that has never been trained to understand what rational conversations look like means you're in trouble.

The second piece I would pass on to parents is that their child's choices are not about them or a reflection on their parenting.

I've seen the best of parents have the worst of kids, and I've seen the worst of parents have the best kids.

I've seen the best of parents lose children to overdose, and I've seen the worst of parents have children that are just incredible, successful people.

The choices our children make are not the by-products of parenting. They're not the result or a reflection of your parenting. I could critique my parenting and say that one of the reasons my son is in this addicted state is because of me not being the dad I could have been.

If I were a bad dad, why are my other two children living incredibly successful, "normal" lives? My son's addiction is not a reflection of bad parenting. All three of my children grew up in the same environment with the same mom and dad. They played sports, and I coached their teams. They had many similar experiences, were exposed to the same teachings, and went through their own personal and challenging experiences. Yet, one got sidetracked into an addiction and the other two didn't. If it were parenting-related, why are two out of three normal?

When moms and dads find out their children are dealing with an addiction, the last thing a mom and dad need to do is make the issue about them. This is a serious issue, and it is not about mom and dad anymore. The addiction is about their child, their child's struggle, their child's illness, and their child's pain.

What parents need to do, right then and there, is to be the mom and dad they need to be for their child, and deal with the issue. This is not a time to feel guilt or shame, or to blame someone and hide from the problem.

Parents need to get the help they need to get support and counseling for their child. They need to be open, honest, and receptive to finding the help needed to get through the crisis.

They need to be willing to work diligently to find the help their child needs, while getting the coaching and counseling they need, as well.

Far too many parents feel too guilty, ashamed, or humiliated to access the help everyone needs to begin working through the issue of substance abuse and addiction. Instead they hole up, try to quietly and secretly take care of the problem, and try to find a cure in the most expedient, efficient way possible. Unfortunately, this is a problem that cannot be quickly, secretly, or easily fixed.

If your child had cancer, would you keep it a secret and deal with it as quickly as possible without doing much research or asking others for guidance or advice? Definitely not. When parents learn their child is struggling with a substance abuse issue, they need to approach dealing with it in much the same way as if their child is taken over by other diseases. Addiction is an illness that is not about mom and dad; instead, it is about giving your child exactly what he or she needs to begin working on getting better.

The third piece of advice is an extension of the second one—understanding the importance of what your child sees and educating him or her from there. Helping children make better choices and decisions stems from understanding what they are seeing, living, and experiencing from a child's view. My advice to parents is to get better at understanding what you need to know about the issues your children face with addiction, bullying, sexual abuse, high sexual activity, drinking, and vandalism. How well do you understand the pressures they feel and experience being a teenager in today's world?

Today's parents are extremely busy. They are focused on growing their careers, protecting or keeping their jobs, maintaining their social status, or competing with the Joneses. There is this external pressure to make sure their child is doing as well in sports, academics, or the social world as the neighbors' kids.

What is most important from a parenting point of view is taking the time to truly understand your child's view, your child's world, the issues that they are facing, and the impact these issues are having on them emotionally, physically, and psychologically. When your child is in a position to safely and comfortably share his or her struggles, fears, and concerns, parents are in a better position to proactively steer him or her away from the adverse external influences.

Being detached, busy, or disengaged, or getting caught up in telling a child what you want him or her to accomplish or achieve doesn't facilitate a safe, trusting teaching environment. When your children can talk to you about the things that they are struggling with, that are causing them pain, and that they find confusing or hurtful it decreases the chance they'll get lost and trust somebody else.

Other Thoughts...
Recovery is a family job. Everyone in the family is responsible for making changes in the recovery process. When everyone is involved in the process, is willing to invest in it, is willing to go through change, and is willing to work to improve his or her communication skills, a loved one has a greater chance of experiencing a sustained recovery.

Far too many parents send their children off to some thirty-day treatment program expecting magical results. Quite frankly, there is no thirty-day treatment program that can deliver the results it promises.

Real, effective, and sustainable treatment and recovery involves two components—at least sixty-to-ninety days in residential treatment and a commitment of loved ones to understand the recovery process, including a willingness to understand and invest in making changes in their habits and behaviors as part of the recovery process.

Approaching recovery with anything less than this level of commitment will result in less-than-desirable results.

You can connect with Dave Cooke on his website at www.100pedals.com.

6

TOUGH LOVE: MY MOST EXCRUCIATING NIGHT AS A PARENT, BY MICHELLE ROSE GILMAN

Note from Cathy: Michelle Rose Gilman is the founder of Fusion Academy, a one-to-one, completely customized middle school and high school, with over forty campuses nationwide. She is the founder of The Well-Heeled Warrior, which is a coaching and mentoring practice for women in business. Michelle also is an artist and owns Feather Punk Studio. She's on the board of directors for Rock to Recovery and the Invisible Disability Project.

More importantly, Michelle is a mother. I came across this story when it was published in the Huffington Post. I stood in my kitchen reading it, tears streaming down my face because I could relate to her story. I reached out to Michelle and she has given her permission to share it here.

During the four months before my son turned eighteen, I think I saw him maybe twelve times. He would leave early in the morning and return late in the evening. When our paths did cross, his eyes were glazed over, his body language screamed eff-you, and he would slink into his room, slam the door, and turn up the music. I knew the drugs were racing through his body and I felt powerless, helpless, and confused. Most of all I was scared to confront him. I was met with lies, fights, yelling, more lies, excuses, and accusations. Addicts are the best liars on earth. Where was my son? How could this have happened? I'd helped thousands of children turn their life around through education and mentoring—why couldn't I help my own son?

I lived in fear that I would get *that* call—the one all parents with kids addicted to drugs fear: that he was either dead or in jail. That call came. He had been arrested. The cops found him passed out in his car, at a stoplight, and they couldn't wake him up. They had to crash the window of the car to rouse him and get him out of the vehicle. Anguish and dread slowly filled my entire body. He wasn't hurt, thank God, but he was stoned out of his mind! He was arrested on the spot and taken to jail. All I could think about after that call was, "Thank God he hadn't killed someone."

But that was not the Most Excruciating Night.

After he was bailed out of jail, his behavior and substance issues got worse. One night I walked to his bedroom. There he was, passed out cold, lights on, with music blaring. My heart was racing, my breath was rapid, and I ran to his bed. I could not wake him up. I yelled, pushed him, and shook his head, all the while screaming his name over and over. He was breathing, but just barely. Just as I was about to sprint out of there to grab my phone and call 9-1-1, he moved, and his eyes slanted open at me. I yelled, "What did you take? Tell me what you are on!" And he told me.

But that was not the Most Excruciating Night.

A few days after that night, he turned eighteen. For the past four months, I had been in contact with addiction specialists, other friends who had navigated this chaos, rehabs, counselors, and anyone who would listen to my story. Mostly I heard, "He has to hit bottom first." I was incredibly grateful for the advice and support I received, but I was still an emotional wreck: constantly sick in my stomach, riddled with anxiety, deprived of sleep, and lost.

And then something came over me that I can only explain as a shock-and-awe epiphany: I couldn't live like this anymore. And at that moment all the emotional shit that I was holding inside of me morphed into a raging burst of epic anger directed at my son. I thought, "You can do this to yourself, but you will not do this to me! Get treatment or get out of my house!"

There would be no more negotiations, no more lies, no more empty threats, no more contracts, no more waiting for him to die in my home! So I gave him the ultimatum — substance treatment or pack your bags and leave this house! At once he knew I was serious. It was not only in my voice, but my conviction was spewing from every cell in my body. My eyes sent darts to his heart. To say he was floored would be an understatement. I could see he was scared to death. But he was addicted, and addicts turn their fear into anger, and he grabbed a backpack, no money to his name, and walked out of the house screaming, "You always mindfuck me!" I pleaded at him, "Please don't make this decision." He kept walking.

But that was not the Most Excruciating Night.

He was gone. One day turned into four days, which turned into more days. I had no idea where he was. I didn't know if he would ever come home and get help. I didn't know if he was alive. I couldn't eat, sleep, or communicate. I tried searching for him to no avail. I was fully absorbed by this experience and the longer this went on, the sicker I became. On the tenth night, around midnight, I heard a light tap at my door.

Here comes the Most Excruciating Night.

"Mom, let me in. Mom, open the door." I was scared to death, my heart beating so hard it felt like tiny earthquakes in my chest. I opened the door slightly. Standing before me was my dirty, stick-thin, pale, sunken-eyed son. "Mom, I need a place to sleep. I'm cold and hungry, please."

As my heart sliced itself up, I looked at him and said, "You don't live here anymore. You made that decision ten days ago. You need to leave." I was turning my own son away at the entrance to our home! What type of sick mother does that? What type of mother can look into the face of her disheveled, filthy, scared son and turn him away?

This type of mother, damn it! I knew I had to do the most excruciating thing ever in order to save my child. It went against every instinct and every fiber of my mom being. Would he turn around and leave again? It was an unbearable risk. The longer he stood there in the sickening silence, the more scared I became. "I'll get help" quietly slipped from his lips, and before I sank to the floor, I opened the door, and he stepped through into the rest of his beautiful life.

A wise person once told me that our kids like their zip codes. They'll come home, but you might first have to endure your most excruciating night.

7

WHERE IS GOD?

Note from Cathy: This chapter is written by a faith-filled mother. The names have been changed; however, her story is as real as it gets.

Where is God? I asked myself this question many times during the years I watched our teenage daughter struggle with alcohol and drugs. The answer is, He was always there in control of the entire journey.

Of course, I asked a lot of other questions too: Why me? What did I do wrong? Why is she doing this to me? What will people think? How do I make her stop? And other self-serving, self-absorbing questions. It was a long and difficult struggle until I finally realized God was using the experience to teach me, my husband, our other daughters, as well as many people we know, lessons we needed to know. For me, the biggest one, and still a daily one, is that I am not in control! It really is about letting go and letting God.

We are a Christian family and have raised our three girls, now twenty-three, twenty-two and sixteen, in the church. Much to my surprise, that did not mean there would not be problems. Ann (not her real name) was born a hefty 9.1 pounds. Within the first week, she was not thriving (the poster child for the chapter in the baby book about the skin hanging from a baby's ankle as a sign of not thriving), and was down to about seven pounds. Two doctors later, we discovered she had a cleft on her soft palate and could not swallow in a normal fashion. We needed to learn a special way to feed her, and she still threw up out of her nose rather than her mouth. At nine months, she had major surgery to repair the cleft and, as she got older, some speech therapy. Had I paid attention, God was there even before she was born. When I moved to Los Angeles eight years earlier, I did volunteer work for an organization known as Women in Show Business, which raised money for children in third-world countries to have cleft repair surgeries at Children's Hospital Los Angeles. Because of my involvement with that group, I had direct access to one of the top surgeons in the country for cleft repair, and we had an appointment within a week.

We learned to feed our daughter, as did the awesome caretakers at her daycare, and she became a strong and fierce, but tiny toddler. Ann was always small, still is at five-two and one-hundred-and-ten pounds dripping wet; but she was tough and feisty. By elementary school, she was becoming a known force on the basketball court and one of the toughest defenders in our local leagues. She usually played up a level, and by fourth grade, was playing club-travel basketball. Her talents continued to develop. In middle school, she played in one of the best-known girls' club basketball programs in the nation, and we traveled around the state and country to tournaments. I spent countless hours driving to and from practices and tournaments with my daughter. But I missed all the signs of trouble ahead...or I just didn't want to admit them.

In middle school, Ann became more and more belligerent toward authority. She got low marks in behavior grades, argued with the teachers, refused to follow the rules, and was kicked off the school basketball team. Rather than identify the problems and begin working on resolutions, I was the fix-it parent, transferring her to a different teacher, disregarding the rudeness to the school coach, making excuses for her, and not learning to parent in a way that she needed.

When she began high school, I began to choose to avoid conflicts with her, again, instead of learning how to parent her in a productive way. She was a starting point guard on the girls' basketball team, and I was so proud of her. But trouble continued to grow and become more serious. We did not have a good relationship. There was a lot of arguing. I failed to hear what she said (I never learned to listen), and I thought she would just grow out of it. She hung out with older girls on the team, some of whom were introducing her to alcohol and drugs. Again, I had my head in the sand and did not see the signs.

By the fall of her sophomore year, she was removed from the basketball team (her passion), and her grades (which were generally always within a 3.0) were below a 2.0. She was hallucinating, not getting along with anyone, lying, disappearing, and losing so much weight that I could see the bones on her shoulders and back. That's what finally led me to take action...the bones. My daughter was dying before my eyes, and I had to fight to save her. I have no idea why it took so long for me to wake up.

The other members of our family were impacted too. My oldest daughter, who attended a rival high school and also played basketball, was terrified of what was happening to her sister and had no way to save her. She made a report to the counselor at her school that she was worried her sister was abusing drugs, and that person contacted the counselor at Ann's school, who contacted a drug-counseling service that comes to the schools—but no one ever contacted us about any of this. My oldest daughter later told me that she would sit in her closet and cry and pray for Ann because of what was happening to her.

Our youngest daughter was horrified by how Ann treated her and us during this time. There was a lot of screaming and cursing at us. Once, Ann took a knife and cut through my head on photos of me and my husband on our refrigerator. Our youngest is five years younger than Ann, and she asked me once if I believed God could talk to us. She was trembling and crying and afraid. I asked why, and she told me that He told her that He wanted Ann to stop what she was doing and that she was supposed to tell her; but she was afraid of her. We all lived in fear, walking on eggshells, worried what we said would send Ann into a nasty, hate-filled cursing tirade at us.

My husband, normally a quiet and sweet man, was a bully parent. He thought if he yelled, she would get it and change her behavior. We fought often over what to do, how to do it, and who was right or wrong. Again, we were in such a state of chaos by then that we never got the message that we needed to learn to be the parents she needed us to be.

We realized that our family was not going to survive if we did not take some action, and our marriage was crumbling. We began seeing a therapist through our church, and she would pray with us. That brought a lot of peace and stability to us and our relationship. I tried to get Ann to go, but she refused, and I could not physically carry her into the sessions. I knew she was depressed and not happy with what she was doing, but too far into it to get out.

That's when we decided we had to send her somewhere for help. I knew if we did not take action before New Year's Eve (we were in December), that she would not live to see another year. I had been put in touch with a woman I knew whose daughter was at a facility in Utah and she thought that would be the place for us. I researched it and talked to the manager of the place. She was all about the money and not that warm and fuzzy. Not thinking we had any other options, my husband and I went to church where, as usual, tears were flowing down my face. That was the only way I worshipped in those days, tears—lots of them—and seemingly empty, unheard prayers. I told my husband I was going to the office to do one more search.

This was the Sunday before Christmas. I searched, as I had many times, and I have no idea what I put into the query, but what I got was a beautiful picture of a peaceful place with large trees on nice grounds, brand new gym/basketball court, kids in their own clothes, and girls with makeup—all of which the other place did not have or allow and which I believed were important to my daughter. It was Shelterwood Academy in Independence, Missouri. We live in California. I read all the information on the site. There was a link to a questionnaire that let you determine whether your family was in need of such a place. I took it. I scored 100 percent. Later, I had my husband take it, and he scored one point less than me. Yes, we needed that help!

Shelterwood was also an accredited school, so she would be able to stay on track and graduate high school on time. It is a Christian school/facility. The best feature was a program where Bigs (young women and men who were recent college grads with sociology/psychology/theology degrees) lived with the students and were mentors. There were group and individual counseling sessions too. I called and spoke with the director, who tried to talk me out of it. He was not concerned about how much money he could make, but rather about whether it was what we needed. He was also concerned that we were having her "taken" rather than willingly bringing her. By the end of our discussion, he realized that was the only way to get her there. I told him we would pray about it and call him soon with our decision.

I left my office and headed to the grocery store. Since it was the Christmas break, there was not much traffic. I was sitting at a large four-way intersection with just me and the car ahead of me. I was lost in thought and tears and looked up to see the license plate in front of me—from Missouri. I went to the grocery store and walked down the paper goods aisle, noticing a very large man in a very loud, blocked shirt, each square a state. And what was staring me in the face as I got closer to him? Missouri. The next night was Monday Night Football, and I watched the Bears play someone. There was an injury time-out. Number ninety-one had Psalm 91 on his face in black. I had been wondering if there was a Bible verse God wanted me to read that would help me, but I never could figure it out. Waiting for the commercials, I decided to look it up...here is Psalm 91: "He who dwells in the *shelter* of the Most High will rest in the shadow of the Almighty. I will say of the Lord, 'He is my refuge and my fortress, my God, in whom I trust'" (emphasis added).

That was all I needed to know that Shelterwood was the right choice. And it was God's way of making sure I understood it was His plan, and that He would protect my child and meet her there.

I called the director and made the arrangements. Another unique part of Shelterwood is that it is a family-inclusive place; in other words, my husband and I had to participate in the intake. I then had to make the hardest plan of all...how we would get Ann there. We planned it for the last weekend of December 2010. I found a transport company and spoke with such a kind person during such a horrible time. He told me that he had transported hundreds of teens over the years, and that one of the places he refuses to take teens is the place in Utah I rejected. Thank you, God, for another save.

We came up with a crazy plan without telling anyone other than our therapist and a friend who was keeping our youngest daughter. I told the kids that I was taking Dad on a surprise trip to Vegas for the weekend, that they were going to stay with friends, and that they could not talk about it. I told Ann nothing. We had a difficult but good Christmas that year, me with many hidden tears, knowing we were all sitting there together and it may very well be the last time. We were at the end of the road. If this plan did not work, I had no backup, no Plan B.

We delivered the oldest and youngest to their respective friends' homes. Ann was with friends at a high school basketball event at her school. I called and told her some convoluted story of the trip to Vegas, that she was going to my business partner's house, that I was coming to get her to take her stuff to the business partner's house, and that, yes, she could go back to the game after that. I already had her bag packed per the instructions of the transport folks and had already packed a suitcase for her that I would take with us. I picked her up at the gym. She was not nice and asked lots of questions about why she had to go to my partner's house instead of her friends', etc. I have no idea how I kept it together in that fifteen-minute car ride other than that God took over. We got home, and she went to her room to get her stuff together. I said I already packed for her and to make sure it was all there.

Within minutes, the transport team, a man and woman I will never forget, came into our house. I took them to her room and told her they were there to take her to a new school where she could get help. She freaked out and lashed out. We were instructed to leave the room. My husband and I huddled in our room, sobbing, praying, hearts breaking, but knowing we had made the right choice and had to go through with it. They got her situated in the back of a car and brought us out to say good-bye. She cursed and said how much she hated us. Then they were gone. We had less than two hours to get our stuff, get to the airport, and catch a different flight to meet them at Shelterwood. Sensing the need for comic relief of sorts, our oldest called and said she forgot her inhaler (she has severe allergies and needs one with her at all times) and my poor husband had to take it over to her without letting her see his sadness and bloodshot eyes. We made our flight, though it is a blur and a nightmare.

When we got to Missouri, the ground was covered in snow. The transport guy stayed in communication with us, letting us know where they were. He was less than an hour ahead of us. We had a rental car, but as we got closer to the school, the snow would not allow us to pass. The director came and picked us up in a jeep for the final five miles or so. The grounds were beautiful. The housing was cabin-like but with large buildings: one for girls, one for boys. We were meeting with the director, the head female Big, our daughter's counselor at the place, and our daughter. It was awful. She was so angry and mean and said horrible things to us, and I was mortified, thinking they were going to send us all away. The director let us know it was a common reaction and that they had heard much worse. After the intake meeting, they took Ann to settle into her room. We were told about the process and payments, told which books we needed to read, and then given a tour. At the end, we were taken to Ann's room to say good-bye. She was asleep, and I woke her to hug her and tell her I loved her. She was so understandably angry. We had to leave not knowing if we would ever see our child again. But God is faithful, and even then, gave me a gift...her Big's name was a version of her best friend's name, and there was a ladybug on the inside of the hall door from Ann's room leading outside. Not only is a ladybug a symbol of good luck, but also a version of that word had been our daughter's nickname her whole life.

I do not know how I got one foot to move in front of the other. We drove back to the airport and flew to Los Angeles, an exhausting twenty-four hour emotional trip. We gathered our other two daughters and explained to them what had happened. They were glad, telling us it was about time we did something. The oldest told us about her fears and about our daughter's drug use. How did I not even know that the balloons in Ann's room were used for drugs? What an idiot I was. The youngest cried and had a lot of questions. I called Ann's basketball coach (she was back on the team, at least for that month, and there was a game the next day). I told him what had happened and he said he would tell the team. He later told me that several girls on the team said they knew Ann was in trouble with what she was doing (i.e., in danger) and he explained how they needed to come to him with such information so the person could be helped. I had to tell my mom and my friends what we had done. Some understood, although questioning the expending of so much money. My response was, "If your child had cancer, you would spend your last penny to save her life," and that is what we were doing.

We then had Ann's friends come over and one of the moms, too. I explained to them what had happened. We all cried. They told me stories of how Ann had tried to harm herself—very serious attempts at death, cries for help I never heard or saw. They were glad we had taken such drastic action, because they did not know how to help her and were very worried about her. Knowing we had made the right decision did not make it any easier.

We were not allowed to talk to Ann for at least three weeks. Then we were allowed short phone calls that were usually about her just telling us how she "fucking hates us". We had one-hour phone-counseling sessions with her therapist at Shelterwood. During her first few weeks there, her roommate slashed her wrists and was taken away in an ambulance. No more makeup mirrors of any type were allowed. Ann heard stories of traumatic events in other girls' lives that she never experienced. She repeatedly told us how we overreacted; she was a normal teenager and did not belong there. It was a year-long program. We made it nine months. By then, there were signs we believed that were indicating she should come home, and we were out of money.

As the Shelterwood folks told us, they do not "fix" your kid, and they do not return to you some perfect kid. I learned so much during that time. Ann studied the love languages book at Shelterwood and shared it with us. Her love language is quality time and words of affirmation. All those times of driving to practices and attending games that I thought were quality time were not to her. I learned from other Shelterwood parents. One of the best things anyone said to me was at the family weekend visit; a mom said, "Don't miss what God is trying to teach you." Boy was he trying to teach me a lot. Some lessons I have learned, and some I'm still learning. My husband learned a lot too, and his relationship with God grew tremendously during this time, leading to his baptism.

Ann came home, graduated high school with honors, and began college. After a year and a quarter, she and we realized she was miserable where she was and she came home to work and finish college online. Every year is a little better. The first few years back, it was two steps forward, one and a half back. It is still hard to watch her struggle or hurt and not be able to stop ourselves from trying to "fix it" so that she doesn't have to feel that pain. I am still learning that one.

Ann has now graduated college. She still struggles with alcohol. She knows she is her best person without it, and when she drinks her relationships suffer. But sometimes, it is just too powerful. We all continue to pray that she keeps fighting that demon. It is now her battle. We cannot fight it for her. We are there to encourage and support her. We also found one of the most wonderful therapists who still sees Ann and others in our family when necessary. Alcoholism is a disease. It ruins lives. God has shown Ann many times and many ways it will ruin her life and her relationships, and she is now voicing an understanding of that. There is always hope.

During the time Ann was abusing drugs and alcohol and acting out in a very disrespectful way toward me in public, I was very embarrassed. I thought others were judging my parenting skills and me as a person by how she behaved, what she said, what she wore, all of it. I had to eat my own words of advice to my daughters to not be concerned about what others think. Those judging me had just as many if not more issues. Some were like me, and didn't even know they had problems. I surrounded myself with supportive women, prayer warriors, who would pray with me and for me and for Ann. Many times, I was joined in her room by one of my praying mom friends, and we would pray for her. I prayed over her when she was home and over her room when she was gone, engaging the devil, telling him she belonged to God and that he would never have her. It was a spiritual battle for my child's soul.

Take all action necessary. Do not refuse to make a tough choice because of fear or because it is hard. That's where God is. He's there in the darkest fear, the toughest choice, the gut-wrenching sobs screamed out in the shower, the pain in the heart for the missing child, the loss of not holding or hugging her…all those places is where I found God. That's what He was teaching me. I am not in control. He is in control. Why did this happen to us? It was our journey. Many other parents have asked for advice and comfort from our story. We are better parents to our youngest daughter and to our two older ones. Ann and I have a fantastic relationship now, and she talks to me about most everything in her life. I wish I had been that person for her years ago, but that was not our role then. She will be an amazing mom and much more in tune with her kids than I from her own walk.

Things I've learned on the journey…

Make sure you do not suggest to your kids that they need to be perfect. There was only one such person and that was Jesus Christ. Make sure your kids know there is nothing they can do that will make you love them any less, just as Christ loves us. Make sure your kids don't think they are a bad person, because they are wonderful people making a bad choice. Learn to listen. Learn the love languages and use your teen's love language. Be present, not five steps ahead to the next place you need to be. We are all too busy and life passes us by. Our kids are stressed and overwhelmed. We are the life raft. We need to be the safe haven, not a place of judgment and condemnation, of demands and competitive expectations. And most of all, get professional help to enhance the communication before it is too late. As the parents, the adults, it is our responsibility to raise these children God has entrusted to us. And yes, teenagers are people, foreign as they may seem. But they are not adults and we cannot expect them to behave as an adult and make decisions with rationale as an adult might.

Parents, do not lose faith or hope. God is always there. Sometimes when you cannot see him or hear him and you are in the darkest dark place, He is the one holding you.

8

THE COUNSELOR'S COUCH: A PROFESSIONAL PERSPECTIVE

Note from Cathy: I have included many perspectives in the book. I firmly believe there is no one-size-fits-all approach. I thought it was important to have a professional perspective as well, although even professional perspectives can be different.

Dr. Nazanin Moali, PhD, is a clinical psychologist specializing in the treatment of addictions and eating disorders. In her private practice in Los Angeles, she has successfully helped many individuals and families struggling with chemical addictions and eating disorders. She is a sought-after speaker and regularly presents at national conferences, in the media, and to professional groups and institutions.

Her blogs and information on her seminars and psychotherapy sessions are available on her website, www.oasis2care.com.

Q: What are the top three reasons you find today's youth turn to drugs and alcohol?

A: Addiction is the result of a complex interaction between a person's genes and their environment. Often times, individuals' genetic predispositions are activated by environmental stressors such as loss and grief, trauma, and separation, which leads to the development of a pathological relationship with various substances. Although there are numerous things that might encourage a youth to turn to drugs and alcohol, below you will find the elements that most frequently facilitate use in my clients.

Self-medication. Numerous studies have highlighted the neurochemical differences in the brains of individuals who have a tendency to use and abuse substances compared to the normative population. For example, in a study by McBride (1995), researchers found a lower level of serotonin in the brains of rats with tendencies to alcohol dependency. Serotonin is a neurotransmitter that regulates mood and sleep, and experiencing mood dysregulation in one's brain chemistry may lead an individual to gravitate toward alcohol and substances.

I often hear from my clients that their abuse of substances got worse when their anxiety, depression, and worries became exacerbated. Many of them started using substances to escape from psychological pain.

The family dynamic Although in many cases parents may not be responsible for the development of a teen's addiction, consciously and unconsciously parents can impact their children's journey to recovery or facilitate substance abuse. For example, teens who start drinking alcohol early (younger than thirteen) have a higher risk of developing alcohol abuse. By not regulating a youth's substance and alcohol use in early childhood and offering them those substances at family gatherings, parents increase their children's chances of developing a substance-use disorder.

Additionally, infants' early experiences of deprivation and maladaptive parent-child interaction influence their coping mechanisms when they become older. Elements such as early physical and sexual abuse, physical illness of a parent, and other traumas may hinder the development of healthy attachment to the primary caregiver, which impact one's ability to effectively manage one's stressors in the environment.

Peer influences. My adolescent clients often identify their relationships with their friends as the most important aspect of their lives. They are often willing to sacrifice many of their values to foster and maintain those relationships. That is a primary reason that when drinking and using becomes prevalent at a school, it turns into an epidemic.

Due to the power of peer influence, many teens with healthy family dynamics and little to no genetic vulnerability may start experimenting with drugs. While a single use often does not translate to a substance-use disorder, it may trigger an addictive cycle if the youth has other vulnerabilities. It is important for school administrators and our communities to closely monitor ongoing trends within this population.

Q: In your opinion, what's the difference between use, abuse, and addiction? How do you know what level a child has reached?
A: There is a continuum of abuse in which abstinence and addiction are two opposite sides. The next step after abstinence is experimentation/use, which is the level where many youths start due to their curiosity and the influence of their peers. At this stage, negative consequences are limited, and many people have no difficulty returning to abstinence, either due to lack of interest or life circumstances.

The next level is abuse, where one starts using substances regardless of the negative consequences one is facing due to their problematic use, such as DUIs, lack of motivation, and missing school/work.

Addiction is the opposite side of the spectrum that shows a lack of control: the addicted person struggles with cutting back. Although many individuals with dependency claim that they are able to reduce or stop their use, often in reality they have difficulty stopping their consumption, due to the severity of their symptoms. At this stage, many people experience multiple serious consequences such as arrests, disrupted relationships, and medical complications, among other things. Additionally, they struggle with cravings and are often preoccupied with thoughts of obtaining and using alcohol and substances. Furthermore, addicted teens have an elevated risk of engaging in hurtful behaviors, such as having unprotected sex, driving under the influence, stealing, and hanging out in unsafe environments.

Q: In your practice, what are the top three things you recommend to a parent when dealing with a youth using/abusing drugs/alcohol?

A: 1. *Establishing clear communication.* This should be the first step with your teen regarding your family rules around substance use. When I initially meet with families for drug counseling, I ask them to define the family rules around drug use in a very clear way and to state the consequences for violating each family rule. Although many parents claim that they have firm rules around drug use, often they have chosen not to implement those rules; this can be confusing to a teen. I recommend discussing the rules with your partner/spouse prior to taking them to your teen. It is essential to appear united in front of your teen so he or she does not take advantage of your different opinions to ignore the rules.

2. *Effective use of consequences.* When choosing consequences for teen substance use, it is crucial to discuss the consequences ahead of time. Many parents decide on the consequence after their teen has violated a rule—and often in the midst of an argument. The downside of waiting until something happens and then deciding on the consequence is that when we are angry, we often come up with consequences that are not practical for the family. These consequences may feel like they punish the entire family. For example, one of my clients violated his curfew and stayed out the entire night during his final days of school. When he got home in the morning, his parents told him that he was grounded for the remainder of the summer, including the use of the car.

Given that he was a senior in high school and was involved in multiple extracurricular activities, it was impossible for his parents to drive him to all his practices since they were both working full time. As a result, his parents ended up giving up on the consequence and returning his car. Setting consequences that are not deliverable often undermines your authority and gives your teen the wrong message about your power as a parent.

3. *Engage in a pleasurable activity as a family.* Combating a teen's substance use can be an exhausting process. Lies and secrets can negatively impact the parent-child relationship and may destroy trust. If you would like to support your teen long-term, it is important to continue engaging in pleasurable activities as a family. Mark days in your calendar to go out and do an enjoyable activity with your teen. During those times, avoid bringing up topics related to substances and keep the conversation less serious. Remember, the focus of these activities is to strengthen your relationship with your teen.

Q: At what point do you suggest a parent make the decision to take action at a higher level (i.e., counseling, local treatment center, sober living, rehab, wilderness)? What are your opinions on the pros/cons of each?

A: If you find yourself repeatedly having the same argument around drug use with your teen, and with limited success, it is crucial to seek out help from a professional mental health provider. Although some parents characterize their teen's use as a "phase," substance use often gets worse as time passes. Sometimes parents perceive asking for help as a sign of failure, so they wait too long to reach out for help, which can drastically impact the treatment outcome. By asking for help when you feel stuck, you can model healthy problem solving for your teen and teach him or her that it is ok to reach out for help.

To find the best level of treatment, you should consider consulting your teen mental health provider as a first step. The fit between client and the facility is one of the main factors contributing to the treatment outcome. Given the cost of inpatient hospitalization, rehab, and wilderness treatment, one must have a clear picture of whether and how a specific program is a good fit prior to sending one's teen to those programs.

Q: If there was only one thing you could tell a parent, what would that be?

A: Regardless of your teen's stage of use and drug of choice, recovery is possible for everyone. I have worked in different facilities with different populations, and I personally witnessed that despite difficult circumstances and if given the necessary tools, people can and do navigate their way out of addiction.

Q: Is there anything else you would like to share to help parents?
A: Abstinence is a midpoint in your teen's journey toward recovery. To create a long-lasting recovery, teens and families need to address the underlying issues that led the teen to use in the first place.

9

LIVING SOBER: A PRESCRIPTION FOR LIFE

Note from Cathy: I recently met Morgan, a young woman who has been in the throws and darkness of addiction. Her story is raw and heartbreaking – YET at the same time, it offers tremendous hope. She is now in recovery and has started a movement for others – Liv SobeRx.

Once upon a time, in a city named Long Beach, along the coast of California, a little girl was born. Her name was Morgan Hunt. From the day I was born I knew I was different. I knew I was meant for something more than the "Average Joe." I also knew I was different from others because I wanted to smoke a cigarette at the age of five and wanted to drink since I knew what alcohol was. I was an alcoholic from the start.

My mother divorced my father as soon as I was born simply because she wanted a child for herself, never realizing the consequences that would follow that choice. A girl without a father is like a lioness without the lion. Every girl needs a great protector whether they believe it or not. For the most part however, I had the perfect childhood - soccer games, sleep overs, and giggles from little girls painted my picture for 8 beautiful years.

The relationship with my father was minimal. He was 6'3, blonde hair, blue eyed, and a Marine. On one occasion while visiting my father, my stepmother gave me alcohol and told me it was ok to drink when there. One evening at the age of 14, as I was getting ready for bed with a glass of Jack Daniels and a cigarette, my step brother came outside to join me. He must have been 38 at the time and saw a fragile broken little girl. He molested me and for the first-time I realized how unprotected I was. Instead of screaming for help, I decided to fake pass out hoping he would leave, which he eventually did. In the morning, I woke up to a screaming household with my father on the phone getting ready to send me back to my mothers. I woke up to a set up. In fear of me telling my father what had happened, my step brother had poured out all the alcohol to make it seem like I drank it all and was obliterated the previous night. I was so enraged and taken aback I couldn't say a word and flew home. This was the first-time I realized it was me against the world.

My stepfather Jim came into my life at age 8 until I was 18. Jim was a wealthy man of statue and power. He owed his own business and had two other children. He had the fancy cars and flashy jewelry but never had love. Even as a little girl at the age of 10, I could see there was no love for me there. My mother was so distracted by all the new exciting and fancy things that she could not see her daughter pulling further and further away. Trips to Paris and remodeling the house seemed to be priority number one.

My mother remarried when I was 14. The marriage was in the Cayman Island so we all took a cruise as a family; my mother, Jim, and my new step brother and sister Mari and Brandon. On that cruise ship, a tragedy happened that would shape my life forever.

"O my God this is going to be so much fun, I have never been on a cruise ship and have no one who cares where I'm at. Let's Get Drunk!", I say to myself. Not understanding the meaning of what I'm saying, I start to get ready and put on a black top and a short white skirt that makes me look way too old for my age. The night begins as I set out by myself to finally have fun, be wanted and feel a part of something. As I'm walking up the stairs to the roof top bar on the top deck, a man of 36 approaches me. "Hi, I'm Anthony, what's your name?" "Morgan", I reply. "Well do you want to get drunk with us?" as he points to his friend. *Sure.* And so, it begins …. my journey with alcohol. Four shots later and I no longer felt 14. I was 21 baby! I was ready to be an adult, or so I thought. Out of everything I can remember that night is one of the worst things I will ever hear. I remember as he shut the door to my room while I'm in tears realizing what just happened to me, he said, "Don't worry. In about a year or so you will be a virgin again." As he slammed the door shut, my heart shut too.

Entering high school that year, I was already a damaged girl with no one to talk to. My mother had moved me away from Long Beach to South Orange County, California, specifically Ladera Ranch. I was my mother's only child and with no siblings or family, all that left for me was my mother and Jim, neither of which wanted to or knew how to talk to a teenage girl about anything at all. I raised myself to the best of my ability with the tools I had already acquired. I was a hard worker, relentless, smart, motivated, and ready to be my own person. I just had absolutely no idea how to get there until I realized I could cope by using drugs and alcohol. At the time, I didn't even realize why I was doing it.

Through high school I received good grades but was constantly in trouble. Because I had good grades, they were not able to kick me out even though they knew I was getting high. Junior year seemed like things were beginning to turn around. I had an attitude adjustment and wanted to be a better person for myself. One of my dreams was always to be able to run confidently in a sports bra. I would be in awe when I'd see the girls running together looking so confident. That year I quit smoking and joined the track team. Most of my teachers didn't believe me when I told them, probably because of my reputation and the fact that they had been hearing me talk about drugs with my friends. It was a good reason not to believe me.

On March 22, 2007, my father died from liver cancer. He contracted it through hep c during his stint in Vietnam for the Marines. Even though we were not that close, it completely rocked my world. Once again, I was completely alone with no one to talk to but myself. Left to my own devices, methamphetamine became my best friend until graduation.

On the day of graduation, I couldn't take living my life that way anymore and broke down to my mother. "I cannot live here anymore" I said. My mother and I packed up my things and I moved back to Long Beach.

Despite all the drug use, I did get accepted into several universities, but I choose California State University Fullerton. The first four years seemed to go well. The drugs stopped and the grades kept getting better, but there was still something missing. It was the same feeling I had felt my whole life – but what was missing. The feeling that I was different never went away. I moved out on my own at age 20. While living in Fullerton, I meet some friends - but one friend that would change my life. Zachary. He was my secret angel in hiding but I wouldn't know that until I was 23.

After 4 years of college, things started to get shaky. When I was about 22, my mother had lost everything; Jim, the house, and the daughter she never had. I got caught up with the wrong people who did the wrong drugs…. OxyContin, which eventually led to heroin. When I tired oxy for the first time, I felt like I could do no wrong. I could never be punished for anything I did and would be loved no matter what happened.

Eventually I got arrested for a DUI but that wasn't enough to for me to stay sober. I had to take that lonely fall down the rabbit hole. Countless nights sitting alone with a needle and spoon wondering when this hell was going to stop. One night, the drugs stopped working. After doing my fix, I felt sober. Completely sober. I started to cry. I cried out for anyone. I cried until I finally cried out for God.

The next day I had 2 warrants and was arrested. I didn't know it then, but God was saving my life. God was doing for me what I could not do for myself. There was no other way that would have worked to get the needle out of my arm. Two years went by as I was trying to fight my case in court, which eventually led up to me just doing my time; a total of 8 months.

When everything was done with the court, I felt as if someone had chewed me up, spit me out then thrown me back into the world. With nowhere to go, I call Zachary who took me in, no questions asked. I had completely forgotten who I was. I had forgotten what I liked to wear, how to do my makeup, and even what kinds of food I liked. I'd forgotten how to smile, laugh, and be a real person. I was broken. I was already defeated inside with shame, guilt, and lack of self-love. How could I function? How could I face the world knowing what I had done and had gone through? Drugs and alcohol were once again my closet friend. I got a job as a bartender in a strip club and started to work and go back to school slowly to the best of my ability. But how can someone excel in school being drunk all the time? It doesn't work. This went on for another year with Zachary, Jameson(whiskey), the strip club, and school. I had some good laughs but never got close to the simple feeling of joy. Joy, peace, and serenity were not in my vocabulary at that point.

In 2016, after an incident at Christmas with a family member, I was thrown over the edge and I couldn't do it anymore. I literally had no energy left spiritually, mentally, or physically. Drugs and alcohol had defeated me and they did not work anymore to take away my pain. Drugs and alcohol could no longer fill that empty hole I had felt my entire life.

"Zachary, I can't do this anymore; I'm going to die. I'm either going to die physically or die from living an average life, just barley getting by on whatever I need for that day. I will eventually die from self-hatred and end up with a gun to my head. I need to stop and I can't do it by myself." I went to a meeting that night and haven't stopped going since.

Life is all about choices. From the day my mother met Jim to what school I attended, it all affected my path and where I am today. I never realized I had the power to take back my life and reclaim my dignity. I am sober today because I have finally chosen to take the right path. I have chosen life over death. I have chosen to be extraordinary and not average. I get to live a successful and meaningful life today - full of real moments with real relationships. Living sober means so much more than just getting rid of the drugs and alcohol. Living sober means being happy, joyous, and free. You have the right to be happy, so take it.

Liv SobeRx is a movement I started – and it's meant to share the message that you never have to be alone again. It's a message that no one must face the world alone, unprotected and hidden. It's not me against the world - it's us with the world. Together we can stay sober by sharing the message that its ok to be an alcoholic. What's not ok is dying from denial. What's not ok is our loved ones dying because they felt they had to keep their alcoholism a secret. I don't believe we should hide in our anonymity anymore. Liv SobeRx is a lifestyle choice that promotes our best selves. Join me in the Liv SobeRx movement and become who you were always meant to be.

Change is all around us every day. The question is when will you make the choice?

You can connect with Morgan at www.LivSobeRx.com.

FINAL THOUGHTS AND MOVING FORWARD

There's a Hole in My Sidewalk: The Romance of Self-Discovery, by Portia Nelson

I walk down the street.
There is a deep hole in the sidewalk.
I fall in.
I am lost...I am helpless.
It isn't my fault.
It takes forever to find a way out.

I walk down the same street.
There is a deep hole in the sidewalk.
I pretend I don't see it.
I fall in again.
I can't believe I am in the same place.
But, it isn't my fault.
It still takes me a long time to get out.

I walk down the same street.
There is a deep hole in the sidewalk.
I see it is there.
I still fall in. It's a habit.
My eyes are open.
I know where I am.
It is my fault. I get out immediately.

> I walk down the same street.
> There is a deep hole in the sidewalk.
> I walk around it.
>
> I walk down another street.

Why do we do the same things over and over and over again expecting different results? Portia Nelson tells the story above. When I first read it, it was obvious. I had fallen into the hole numerous times. I'd been in the hole with my son, I've been in the hole with relationships, and I was most recently in the hole with a friendship. The hole for me is codependency. I am now walking another street, which may or may not have a hole, but I'm aware of my steps.

For me, 2017 is a year of new beginnings: a new career, a new life, and a new outlook. Since beginning to write this book in 2015, I have gone in a different direction from my husband; we divorced after twenty-nine years of marriage. I am so incredibly grateful we weathered the storm of drug abuse together. I am blessed that we have an amicable relationship after divorce and our kids are still our first priority.

While divorce was not on my life plan, I've come to understand life has many peaks and valleys, ups and downs, and moving through them with grace and gratitude is the only way to survive. Over the last few years, I have been humbled. And while I wouldn't wish this nightmare on anyone, I am a stronger woman for it.

There are numerous lessons I've learned through my journey, but I'll share the top three:

1. *Everyone is facing a challenge.* While in the beginning I felt like the only mother who had ever faced such a thing, as I began talking about it, others began sharing their journeys with me. It was clear that the "perfect mom" wasn't so perfect, after all, and that we all are facing challenges big and small. But if we are willing to be vulnerable and share our challenges, the support, love and understanding far outweigh the shame.
2. *Faith is not faith until it is acted on.* Faith is defined on Dictionary.com as "confidence or trust in another person" and "belief that is not based on proof"—and of course, "belief in God or a Higher Power." For me, my faith centers around my belief in God. But whatever your faith is, are you acting on it? We talk about taking a leap of faith in our lives, but so many of us hold back and don't step up. We aren't willing to take that leap because we are afraid of the fall. But I would like to suggest that we won't grow without taking that leap; and the lessons learned when we fall are some of the most important lessons in life. Those lessons are what move us forward.
3. *There is always a lesson to be learned—and until you learn it, it will keep showing up.* You may think you got it, you may think you understand, but until you truly do, the lesson has a funny way of repeating itself…over, and over, and over again. Through being aware and open to the lessons, I have found a huge sense of peace. I'm not saying that I don't have a lot of lessons I'm still learning and that they aren't painful, but what I am saying is

I am open to them and by working through them and not trying to avoid them, I am happier, more content, and fulfilled.

I know my God-given purpose and mission is to serve families facing abuse and addiction. I'm doing this within my life and recovery-coaching practice, speaking publicly about my experience through addiction, codependency, and recovery—and writing this book.

On that note, I also want to thank my son for giving me permission to share our story. He is an amazing young man with a bright future – a man I am very proud to call my son. He has always understood my desire to share the story in hopes of helping others—and he shares that hope with me.

My faith in God has seen me through some very dark, difficult times, and He continues to walk the journey with me. I pray every day to inspire other mothers through my story, to help them know they are not alone, to help them know that they must let go of the shame and come together as a community to help our society face and understand the stigma of addiction.

There is hope. You are never alone.

APPENDIX: RESOURCES

There are many resources I used, as well as others I have learned about since starting my journey. As resources are always changing and new ones come about, you can visit my website and download the current list: www.CathyAlessandra.com/RecoveryResources.

CONNECT WITH CATHY

Cathy Alessandra is a Certified Professional Life and Recovery Coach. She helps her clients by peeling back the layers to discover what drives them, what motivates them, and what makes them see the world the way they do; she helps them make the necessary shifts for a positive, fulfilling, joy-filled life. Cathy uses her twenty-plus years of entrepreneurial experience along with her journey of self-discovery and transformation through life's challenges to provide her clients and audiences solid takeaways and strategies.

Cathy is the CEO of Alessandra Group LLC and founder of the Yes I Can and ReDirect Life programs. She is an Associate Certified Coach (ACC) with the International Coach Federation as well as a Certified Professional Recovery Coach with the International Association of Professional Recovery Coaches. She has been featured on CBS.com, career-intelligence.com, and KFWB news radio in Los Angeles, among others. She has received many awards for her work in business and has received the President's Call to Service Life-Time Achievement award for her philanthropic endeavors.

To connect further with Cathy, visit www.CathyAlessandra.com.

Made in the USA
San Bernardino, CA
23 March 2018